First edition, October 2008

Vitally Important Books
www.vitallyimportant.com

SAN: 257-6252
ISBN: 978-0-9774807-2-2

The Do-It-Yourself Constitutional Amendment Kit.

by Nathaniel Whitten

A true patriot herself, Ms. Washington rode shotgun on her husband' military, political, and personal horse for four decades. Her sacrifice set the standard for all first ladies (and gentlemen) to follow.

Dedicated to John, Paul, George, and Martha.

We humbly thank our forefathers and mothers from Olde Philadelphia who risked life and limb to create a more perfect union. Special gratitude to the 39 signers of the Constitution for putting pen to parchment before they were tempted with lavish gifts and golf outings by those with "special interests."

Tom says:

"No society can make a perpetual constitution, or a perpetual law. The earth belongs always to the living generation. Every constitution, then, and every law, naturally expires at the end of 19 years. If it be enforced longer, it is an act of force and not of right."

We the actual people,

who do not claim to be senators, or lobbyists, or superdelegates, or even local school board administrators, but simply concerned citizens who wish to see these United States of America survive and thrive beyond our short time here on earth, hereby declare that we're stepping in to restore a level of decency, intelligence and trust in our democracy that's gone missing in recent years. (If you've seen it, please call 1-202-456-1111*.)

Despite employing nine million of us in some form of federal, state, or local job to protect and to serve, we now find our system of checks and balances shaken to core due to the following: an excess of prosperity and power clutched in the hands of the few; dismissal of diplomacy in favor of fear-mongering and jingoism; an overwhelming dependency on foreign oil and outsourced labor, and too much corporate influence directing too many votes in the halls of Congress. (Okay, so you might want to consider this a short list.)

Meanwhile, the freedoms we claim as our "God-given rights" are quietly being rescinded, as we find they are no more God-given here then they are in Syria, Iran, or North Korea.

---

*White House switchboard

To think that Adams and Franklin and Morris all put their lives on the line so that we could be held hostage by multi-national corporations and sovereign wealth funds is an odd notion indeed. Therefore, to ensure our democracy stays solvent, as well as accountable, it is imperative that we follow the instructions left us by the Founding Fathers.

According to Jefferson and company, each succeeding generation is supposed to improve the strength and transparency of government by revising the Constitution to reflect our evolution as a species. Tom and George, James and John Quincy – these gentlemen knew the world wasn't going to stand still. Whether they envisioned semi-automatic machine guns, flat screen televisions and $6 cups of coffee is another question.

Change will not be easy. Most of our politicians are trained as lawyers, which make them doubly dangerous in how they interpret the law. Notice how they refer to the Constitution as a "sacred document" in order to provide excuses for their myopia and inflexibility.

By shielding themselves behind a 200-year-old piece of faded parchment, they can continue to plunder and pillage rather than make certain next year's crop of taxpayers inherits a stronger, more trust-worthy system.

But one thing they can't ignore is numbers, whether from a CNN/Harris poll or the outpouring of citizens who won't let their latest indiscretions stand as examples of responsible government.

And so let us rise up with the force of 300 million strong and intercede before our democracy winds up on the scrapheap of "noble experiments." Now is the time to right our lilting ship, set a positive example for other nations, and not burn like Rome with the last of our fossil fuels thrown on for good measure.

Signed,

Note: some signers of important documents like to write in large, scripty type. So we've allowed for plenty of space for your "John Hancock."

Edmund Randolph, George Mason and Elbridge Gery refused to sign the original Constitution due to the lack of a bill of rights. In retrospect, a very smart move.

Let the word go forth:

A few sample

Constitutional Amendments,

to get you started on the road

to a more perfect union.

The following are intended to instigate discussion
and debate, and ultimately help inspire your own
suggestions for how to improve our democracy.
Feel free to rewrite any you violently disagree with,
or add on to those you find to your liking.

Proposed Amendment XXVIII:

"Commander in Chief" title taken literally, not subjectively.

If a war is truly worth waging, the call to sacrifice shall be shared from top to bottom.

Therefore, should a President of the United States declare war upon another country, state, or private residence due to his conviction that it's in the best interests of our country, that President will be required to physically lead the charge into battle.

No longer will the Chief Executive give an address from the Oval Office sending our troops into harm's way, and then retreat to the comfort of the Lincoln Bedroom to watch the game of the week on ESPN. Day One of any invasion, the President will be at the front lines, commanding the troops and directing the generals who report to him.

Moreover, the President's family, including his or her offspring, spouse, parents (if living) and any first and second cousins will also be immediately sworn in as active members of the armed forces and be assigned forthwith. All shall serve no less than six months and no more than two years as first responders, carrying out the military plans of their blood relative, known as "Mr. President" to us but by some odd nickname like "Pajama Pants" or "H" by those closest to him.

The example set by the President and his family will send a heroic message to the rest of our citizenry, as well as to the world, that we are not hypocrites, but believe in "the mission," whatever it may be.

While president, he squeezed into his old uniform and went off to quell The Whiskey Rebellion. Back then, it was known as "leading by example."

The Almighty prefers to remain media-neutral and
non-partisan. (Note: this is a representation of Zeus.
Everyone has their own conception of God; nobody
is 100% sure what the All-Powerful actually looks
like.)

Proposed Amendment XXIX:

God is great (and is also happiest when out of the political spotlight).

Despite a huge contingent who would like our country to be run on a platform of Christian doctrine (or Jewish, or Baptist, or Buddhist), we must not pander to elements that will take our focus off what's truly important in favor of side issues , i.e. "God likes us better" or "God told me to bomb Bagdhad."

God is a concept that is not ownable by our president or even our nation, just as it is not owned by any prime minister, emperor, Royal Family, judge, alderman, or dictator. God is better than that, and to behave as if God wants one nation to have three cars in every garage, while another should be riddled with famine and disease, is both foolhardy and unwise. Especially given that history has turned the tides on seemingly invincible powers often enough to never take for granted the hard work that's required to keep a government moving forward, rather than back.

Henceforth, any person running for office who brings up such issues will be automatically disqualified, in order to make way for secular decision makers who do not cast votes based on sacred observance. So help us God.

Proposed Amendment XXX:

Minimum age requirement dropped to 18 to run for office. Any office.

Eighteen-year-olds can go to war, get married, adopt children, sign legal documents, even develop a computer software program that changes the face of business. So why can't they run for elected office? Besides, with all the chemicals in our food accelerating puberty in adolescents, they're ready to lead much earlier than the forefathers had previously deemed responsible.

However, in order to appease the elders who think grey hair means "wise" and not "doddering", a mathematical formula will be instituted to ensure that youth will be balanced by experience. Thus, the elected official's cabinet, inner circle, or pages must average up to a median age of 48. Example: If 21-year-old Larry is voted Senator from Maine, his two assistants must be 57 and 66 to achieve quorum.

Proposed Amendment XXXI:

Ralph Nader given consolation prize in exchange for never running again.

The tradition of third party candidates for public office, whether they be from the Green Party, The Libertarians, The Masons, or The Freaks, is of immense importance to our health as a democracy. Yet some guys just don't know when to throw their hat out of the ring. So while third party candidates shall be welcome in all elections great and small, after an individual has run for office and received at least 3% of the popular vote, they will be given an honorary position in the President's cabinet so long as they pass the torch and don't run ever again.

Unreasonable men and women are
vital to our democracy, and should be
honored for refusing to "toe the line."

Proposed Amendment XXXII:

Right to bear arms, so long as they're muskets.

The reasons our founding fathers originally gave citizens the legal recourse to arm themselves were three-fold: no home burglar alarms, no state and local police, and no semi-automatic weapons. Loading a musket required a 30-second process (see "instructions"), which enabled a hothead to cool down while he stuffed the powder in the chamber; hence, fewer regrettable homicides. If ever there was an area where we should bring our thinking up to the present, it's this one.

So for those who are not serving in the armed services, or patrolling our land as members of a police unit, guns modeled after those from the 1700s will be available, provided a license is applied for and a full check of their mental faculties is conducted before issuing a permit.

Instructions for loading and firing (abridged)

"Prime and load." Make a quarter turn to the right at the same time bringing the musket to the priming position. The pan opens following the discharge of the previous shot, the frizzen would already be up. "Handle Cartridge." Draw a cartridge. Cartridges consist of a spherical lead bullet wrapped in a paper cartridge which also holds the gunpowder propellant. The other end of the cartridge away from the ball should be sealed with a twist of paper. Rip off the paper end of the cartridge and throw it away, keeping the main end with the bullet in your right hand.
"Prime." Pull the dogshead back to half-cock and pour a small pinch of the powder from the cartridge into the priming pan. Then close the frizzen so that the priming powder is trapped.
"About." The butt of the musket is then dropped to the ground; pour the rest of the powder from the cartridge, followed by the ball and paper cartridge case into the barrel. This paper acts as wadding to stop the ball and powder from falling out if the muzzle is declined.
"Draw ramrods." Draw your ramrod from below the barrel. First force it half out before seizing it backhanded in the middle, followed by drawing it entirely out while simultaneously turning it to the front and placing it one inch into the barrel.
"Ram down the cartridge." Use the ramrod to firmly ram the wadding, bullet, and powder down to the bottom followed by tamping it down with two quick strokes. The ramrod is then returned to its hoops under the barrel.
"Present." The butt is brought back up to the shoulder. You pull the cock back and the musket is ready to fire.

Proposed Amendment XXXIII:

Majority rule.
(You'd think this would go
without saying.)

The electoral college may have been a wise idea 100 years ago, but today it's a prop for giving Ohio, Indiana, and Florida the power to pick our President every four years. Let's eliminate this archaic system designed to give equal weight to all the states back when there were only 15, and create a populist system that tallies one person, one vote.

Just as our citizens are free to decide where to live, their vote should be counted equally in deciding who to nominate and elect as their leader. No gerrymandering and back room bias should interfere with this rule, including ex-chief executives stumping for their spouses in the primaries.

Proposed Amendment XXXIV:

Have at least one eight-year-old in the presidential cabinet.

Eight-year-olds have interesting ideas.

Eight-year-olds tell the truth, unless they've spilled something, in which case they point to the person sitting next to them.

Eight-year-olds are almost always for more peace and less war.

Eight-year-olds have not had the soul sucked out of them by the political process.

Eight-year-olds know when it's time to take a break for Wall Ball.

Proposed Amendment XXXV:

When duty calls, it shouldn't go to voicemail.

All who are born and raised under the stars and stripes are granted a privilege that seven out of ten people in the world would (and often do) die for. Yet many of us have come to take this for granted – nay, believe it is our right to live in freedom while others are crushed under the weight of despotism or religious inflexibility. We have lately been told our primary duties as American citizens are to make money, buy real estate at inflated prices, and rack up credit card debt as fast as our APRs will let us.

To readjust priorities, it is now deemed that every citizen who is over the age of 18 shall be available for duty to their country for a period of two years, to be spread evenly between peacekeeping, social work, helping those less fortunate, or in general being useful to someone other than themselves in whatever way is deemed the strongest use of their skill set. A standardized test will be administered in the junior year of high school to determine the proper placement.

Armed forces service shall be determined by lottery in times of necessity, and no deferments will be permitted for any reason. Thus, going to battle will not be limited to low-income men and women who lack either white collar career opportunities or connections to the rich and powerful who can wangle favors to get them off the hook.

Many of the powerful who defend the National Rifle Association and lobby for military action over diplomacy received deferments from the armed forces. We can't ask others to defend what we refuse to do ourselves.

Proposed Amendment XXXVI:

Ensuring Strom Thurmond doesn't run again, even though he's dead.

Obviously, the longer you're in Washington, the more comfortable you get with the Beltway. As Senator Robert Byrd said regarding his run for a record-setting ninth term in office, "I've got a head up here that hasn't changed one iota in the last 25 years." Hmmm.

Some 200 years ago, the leaders of the U.S.A. could have never foreseen an election process as rigged, biased, and slanted towards the incumbent as it is today, Meanwhile, every four years our elections cost in excess of $3 billion dollars, enough to build at least three more overpriced sports stadiums (or help our poorest citizens afford food and shelter).

From this moment forward, term limits shall be instituted so that politicians serve no more than 12 years in office. In addition, all PAC dough and soft money will no longer go directly to a campaign or a commercial. Instead, each candidate will be assigned a governmental agency in need of funding, such as education, agriculture, alternative energy, and social security. All contributions will go to funding better infrastructure, while being attributed to the candidate so they can benefit from the association in the eyes of the voters.

48 years in the Senate. Was Machiavelli right?

Proposed Amendment XXXVII:

Disqualify the lawyers.

Surely they may serve their country by advising the candidates and office-holders. But to rely upon those whose ability is gauged on interpreting the rules rather than modernizing them is one reason we're always up a creek without a canoe, much less a paddle.

How many lawyers does it take
to cross-examine one of these?

Proposed Amendment XXXVIII:

No voter? No motor.

No longer shall voting be a "well, I was gonna go to the polls but it was raining and I had to pick up Michelle from soccer practice" type of exercise. Voting is a privilege that other countries wish they had. If voting came with a free salad spinner, you'd see a crush of bodies at 7 a.m. at every polling station in the country. So here's what we're going to do: no driver's license shall be issued or renewed unless the person in question has voted in that year's election. While the results might wind up the same, the participation won't.

A sweet ride. But you'll need
to cast a ballot to drive it.

Proposed Amendment XXXIX:

Political speeches:
14 minutes maximum.

JFK's inaugural address clocked in at a scant 13 minutes 45 seconds, yet had more memorable sound bites in it that all the stemwinders from Clinton, Nixon, and Reagan combined.

Unless there's a purpose for the long-winded and obtuse, why not shoot for more eloquence and less bombast. Remember, George Washington's second inaugural address was the shortest on record—just 135 words— and he was the Father of Our Country. Let's respect the citizens' schedules, not take them hostage.

"Ask not what your country can do for you..." first appeared in Kahlil Gibran's Open Letter to Lebanese Nationalists in about 1915. Better to filch a great thought than pen a bad one.

Proposed Amendment XL:

Fair Tax to be rendered immediately. (Steve Forbes, take a bow.)

Look, even the mega-rich are embarrassed at this point by the division of wealth in this country. It's all well and good to say you've "worked hard for the money," but people who enjoy working hard will do so even if they are taxed as harshly as the lazy waiter who has forgotten their roquefort at the local steak house.

Therefore, without further debate, a "fair tax" shall be instituted which will be 20% across the board. No write-offs, no shelters, no "hey, look at this hand while I stick my money in Switzerland with this other hand." Rich and not so rich, 20%.

This will save the government approximately $50 billion a year in IRS employees, while they collect an estimated $300 billion in additional revenues. Not a bad thing, considering we're only $44 trillion in debt. That's $100,000 for every man, woman, child, and farm animal in this country.

Proposed Amendment XLI:

Private enterprise and public good: now one and the same.

Our democracy is overweighted in the corporate structure first created by Britain in the 1600s. This was intended to encourage economic growth in the new world. It obviously has worked a little too well.

Now bloated and unseemly, we must police our industries with the same zeal we searched for communists in show business during the McCarthy era. Especially because fully 61% of all Americans own shares of publicly traded stocks which are affected by the honesty and truthfulness of the individuals running said companies.

Free markets are a good thing. Chief executives and boards of directors who operate above the law and make colossal errors of judgement without fear of reprisals are not. For them to be rewarded for reckless behavior with golden parachutes rather than jail sentences shall no longer be condoned under the "rich get richer" code of silence. After all, no workers get bonuses after they screw up and mistakenly solder a car trunk shut, or put mouse droppings in the soup tureen.

Thus, it is time we organized better oversight to discourage shenanigans at the highest levels of private enterprise which have become as important to our nation's strength and fortitude as anything occurring on Capitol Hill.

Starting in the next fiscal year, all top managers of publicly held enterprises will be remunerated based on the annual stock performance of the 72-year-old retiree who buys 100 shares of their company on the open market.

In addition, CEOs shall be forced to give back any and all gains if their companies find themselves in a compromised position due to shoddy accounting. Should their performance be particularly heinous, said CEO will be placed in stockades in a public square (or corporate office park) for no less than 90 days so that they may feel the wrath of shareholders who got burned from their disappointing leadership.

JP Morgan. What would he think
of the financial system today?

Proposed Amendment XLII:

No cell phone usage on public transportation.

It is obvious that: a) the people with the least to say are the ones who spend the most time talking on their cell phones and: b) they have no regard for the ears of those around them since they do not attempt to whisper, muffle, or in any way dampen the abrasive sound of their screeching laughs or gutteral emissions, especially in crowded areas such as commuter trains where other passengers cannot escape their natterings about babysitters, social engagements, real estate prices, or their upcoming surgeries.

Thus, we hereby rescind the freedom to use portable phones in areas wherever two or more commuters are gathered. If one is caught using said device other than in a legitimate emergency, we hereby grant the freedom for any person placed in earshot to snatch the phone from the hand of the mannerless windbag and crush it with the full force of their boot heel. Slapping the person in the face with a glove is also allowed (one slap per minute of usage).

Common decency is a cornerstone of common good. Bringing back manners as a matter of course will go a long way towards shoring up our tattered empire.

Torture shall be expressly forbidden, except for loud public users of cell phones, in which case it's perfectly reasonable to teach them a lesson.

Proposed Amendment XLIII:

Equal representation per dollar of taxation.

Currently all 50 states get two senators each, whether they have populations the size of Vermont or Texas. Not to disrespect Vermont, but most residents are forced to move from there the minute they reach adulthood in order to find jobs other than that of Ben & Jerry factory tour guide.

Consider also Montana, North Dakota, and New Mexico. All are granted two senators apiece, yet total population of the three states combined still doesn't equal that of Ohio. This is not what the Founders intended when they crunched the numbers for Congress based on population in 1787, not 2007. Back then, almost everyone resided in the greater northeast and no state had more than a million residents.

Today, based on this unfair distribution of public servants, just 17% of the population can sway the majority opinion rendered in the Senate We hereby call for a recount. But rather than take away Senators from the smaller states (they will go ballistic and most of their residents are armed to the teeth), we hereby propose that larger states gain additional senatorial representation based on population density and tax burden. The same goes for the House.

And to think they both get two senators apiece.

Population: 683,478   Population: 36,553,213

This would create a fairer and more equitable representation of the people, who should not be penalized for living in areas where they can actually travel via public transportation rather than driving large trucks that get seven miles to the gallon.

Proposed Amendment XLIV:

Reading. Writing. Then running.

All candidates for public office of any sort, be it Congress, Senate, or the Presidency, will be required to read at least 20 books determined by a quorum of scholars assembled from private and public universities. Ovid, Plato, Aristotle, J.D. Salinger, and Charles Bukowski shall be included in the syllabus.

This dovetails nicely into Part Two of this Amendment: that candidates and public officials be made to write their own speeches. This way, the voters can determine which of those standing before the phalanx of microphones is capable, intelligent, and understandable, versus an empty suit being manipulated by others for the good of their party. The ability of our leaders to speak with clarity and conviction, and rouse the country to shared sacrifice, shall be a prerequisite and not a bonus.

A little "Jane Eyre" can go a long way.

Proposed Amendment XLV:

Develop an iTunes store for democracy.

Since Steve Jobs and friends operate one of the few enterprises left in the America that is focused on quality, modernity, and democratic principles, we propose that they be given a federal grant to create software that would allow our citizenry to securely vote on issues before the people -- while waiting for their movies to finish downloading.

Call it iDemocracy, or MacPopulace, or whatever. But placing our freedoms in the hands of technologically advanced computer manufacturers that put smart design first is a much better idea than trusting voting machines to make accurate tallies. Eventually, we can abolish Congress in favor of individual internet representation.

The political system for the rest of us.

Proposed Amendment XLVI:

Marriage between any two (or more) consenting adults fine and dandy.

Liberty and justice for all shouldn't stop at the altar. So enough with the judgments of fallible humans masquerading as our moral adjudicators. Same sex? Fine. Opposite sex? Fine too. Threesome? Quadrangle? Eight-way? Suit yourself. Just pay your taxes on time, live and let live.*

The key word is "consenting."

*Note: this includes Mississippi.

Proposed Amendment XLVII:

Extra checks and balances formed with new "Fifth Estate Lotto."

Since government time and again has proved its inadequacy at properly addressing the needs of the people, it is time to create a true "vox populi" to provide an adequate counterweight to our three-tiered system of government, and the fourth estate that covers them.

We love lotteries in this country; therefore every taxpaying citizen will be entered into the "Fifth Estate Lotto", with two people from each of the 50 states chosen at random to serve a four-year term. They will be given a leave of absence from their jobs, and continue to be paid salaries commensurate with what they were making at the time of their selection. They will be put up at a three-star hotel paid for by the Hilton family as payback for not raising their daughters in a manner respectful of the country, and be called upon to rule without prejudice in cases where Congress becomes deadlocked, or in manners of impeachment, or deciding whether to go to war after a President has declared it.

Proposed Amendment XLVIII:

No more appearances on comedy shows by those running for office.

For aspirants to the nation's highest office to go on talk shows and play the fool diminishes the gravity of the position which they seek. The respect we should accord our leader evaporates with every lame joke they telegraph.

Playing bass guitar with the "Tonight Show" band or doing magic tricks for the hosts of "The View" is wonderful, but has become more important than the candidates' stand on economic issues and national defense. Yet the practice continues due to the free media coverage the candidates garner for being perceived as "one of the gang, in on the joke, hey did you hear the one about the dictator and the pile of hush money?" Let's keep our stand-ups and our world leaders separate from here on out, to restore dignity to the office and officeholders alike.

Proposed Amendment XLIX:

Move the inauguration indoors.

Since it's usually colder than a witch's mammary on January 20th, the ceremony of swearing in our Presidents shall take place in the Capitol Rotunda. Free coffee and hot chocolate will be served to the first 10,000 in attendance.

Remember the ninth president of the United States? Neither do most people. William Henry Harrison caught a chill at his inauguration and died a month later. His two-hour speech might have had something to do with it (refer to Amendment XXXIX).

Proposed Amendment L:

Just say "yes" to tax revenues from pleasure drugs.

As people enjoy getting stoned as an adjunct to getting liquored up, and as the government could make some real money legislating the sale of recreational substances by taxing them, rather than spending billions in the "war on drugs" and locking up thousands busted for a minor infractions, we hereby declare that marijuana shall be legalized and become a revenue generator for our country.

Should the legalization of "smoke" prove successful, this will be a first step towards the legalization of recreational drugs in their entirety, which will be distributed in state-licensed stores called "Happy Houses" and provide another shot in the arm to states looking for additional revenue.

Overcrowded prisons will no longer be needed to house drug offenders, and will be sold to private enterprise to be turned into opera houses, skateboard parks, or rehabs.

Proposed Amendment LI:

On the addition of extra states to the union.

Any country that wants to become an official state of the union may join assuming they are a democracy, can bring at least $100 billion in annual revenue to the table, and don't mind sharing a federal government.

In the case of changing number of stars in the flag, the sewing job shall be bid out to American manufacturers first, then the Taiwanese.

Any government official who has castigated others publicly for the same lifestyle they pursue privately should strive for a more secretive location to woo their paramours.

Proposed Amendment LII:

Personal lives of public officials off-limits. Unless they involve lobbyists, spies, or airport men's rooms.

Our lurid fascination with politicians as they seek a little pleasure after hours does little to forward democracy. If they want to cross-dress and be whipped on their own time, so be it. This shall be kept out of the headlines by our fourth estate, who practiced admirable restraint during Kennedy's time. Reporters can go back to pursuing stories that help foster good government, rather than dime-store headlines.

However, should one's hedonistic pursuits be counter to his public proclamations of moral righteousness, then all bets are off and he should be immediately ejected from office and his parking pass revoked.

Proposed Amendment LIII:

Requirement of all citizens to read the Constitution. (Handy copy provided).

As one needs a license to get married, or own a gun, or operate a Vespa, so should a license be required to be a qualified citizen of the United States.

This way, every adult will be aware of their rights, their responsibilities, and their good fortune in being born here and not in Kazakhstan. Also, they can better participate in the public discourse concerning matters political in nature and be able to point out when their individual rights, or rights are a group, are being violated.

A written test will be given to individuals when they reach 16 years of age, to be called "Hey, I Get It Now," and this will prepare all citizens of the U.S. to vote with full understanding in future elections.

Appendix

Number One:

The Constitution as

it currently stands.

(Not bad, but in need of improvement.)

We the People of the United States, in Order to form a more perfect Union, establish Justice, insure domestic Tranquility, provide for the common defence, promote the general Welfare, and secure the Blessings of Liberty to ourselves and our Posterity, do ordain and establish this Constitution for the United States of America.

Article. I.
Section. 1.
All legislative Powers herein granted shall be vested in a Congress of the United States, which shall consist of a Senate and House of Representatives.

Section. 2.
The House of Representatives shall be composed of Members chosen every second Year by the People of the several States, and the Electors in each State shall have the Qualifications requisite for Electors of the most numerous Branch of the State Legislature.

No Person shall be a Representative who shall not have attained to the Age of twenty five Years, and been seven Years a Citizen of the United States, and who shall not, when elected, be an Inhabitant of that State in which he shall be chosen.

Representatives and direct Taxes shall be apportioned among the several States which may be included within this Union, according to their respective Numbers, which shall be determined by adding to the whole Number of free Persons, including those bound to Service for a Term of Years, and excluding Indians not taxed, three fifths of all other Persons. The actual

Enumeration shall be made within three Years after the first Meeting of the Congress of the United States, and within every subsequent Term of ten Years, in such Manner as they shall by Law direct. The Number of Representatives shall not exceed one for every thirty Thousand, but each State shall have at Least one Representative; and until such enumeration shall be made, the State of New Hampshire shall be entitled to chuse three, Massachusetts eight, Rhode-Island and Providence Plantations one, Connecticut five, New-York six, New Jersey four, Pennsylvania eight, Delaware one, Maryland six, Virginia ten, North Carolina five, South Carolina five, and Georgia three.

When vacancies happen in the Representation from any State, the Executive Authority thereof shall issue ' Writs of Election to fill such Vacancies.

The House of Representatives shall chuse their Speaker and other Officers; and shall have the sole Power of Impeachment.

Section. 3.

The Senate of the United States shall be composed of two Senators from each State, chosen by the Legislature thereof for six Years; and each Senator shall have one Vote.

Immediately after they shall be assembled in Consequence of the first Election, they shall be divided as equally as may be into three Classes. The Seats of the Senators of the first Class shall be vacated at the Expiration of the second Year, of the second Class at the Expiration of the fourth Year, and of the third Class at the Expiration of the sixth Year, so that one third may be chosen every second Year; and if Vacancies happen by Resignation, or otherwise, during the Recess of the Legislature of any State, the Executive thereof may make temporary Appointments until the next Meeting of the Legislature, which shall then fill such Vacancies.

No Person shall be a Senator who shall not have attained to the Age of thirty Years, and been nine Years a Citizen of the United States, and who shall not, when elected, be an Inhabitant of that State for which he shall be chosen.

The Vice President of the United States shall be President of the Senate, but shall have no Vote, unless they be equally divided.

The Senate shall chuse their other Officers, and also a President pro tempore, in the Absence of the Vice President, or when he shall exercise the Office of President of the United States.

The Senate shall have the sole Power to try all Impeachments. When sitting for that Purpose, they shall be on Oath or Affirmation. When the President of the United States is tried, the Chief Justice shall preside: And no Person shall be convicted without the Concurrence of two thirds of the Members present.
Judgment in Cases of Impeachment shall not extend further than to removal from Office, and disqualification to hold and enjoy any Office of honor, Trust or Profit under the United States: but the Party convicted shall nevertheless be liable and subject to Indictment, Trial, Judgment and Punishment, according to Law.

Section. 4.
The Times, Places and Manner of holding Elections for Senators and Representatives, shall be prescribed in each State by the Legislature thereof; but the

Congress may at any time by Law make or alter such Regulations, except as to the Places of chusing Senators.

The Congress shall assemble at least once in every Year, and such Meeting shall be on the first Monday in December, unless they shall by Law appoint a different Day.

Section. 5.
Each House shall be the Judge of the Elections, Returns and Qualifications of its own Members, and a Majority of each shall constitute a Quorum to do Business; but a smaller Number may adjourn from day to day, and may be authorized to compel the Attendance of absent Members, in such Manner, and under such Penalties as each House may provide.

Each House may determine the Rules of its Proceedings, punish its Members for disorderly Behaviour, and, with the Concurrence of two thirds, expel a Member.

Each House shall keep a Journal of its Proceedings, and from time to time publish the same, excepting such Parts as may in their Judgment require Secrecy; and the Yeas and Nays of the Members of either House on any question shall, at the Desire of one fifth of those Present, be entered on the Journal.

Neither House, during the Session of Congress, shall, without the Consent of the other, adjourn for more than three days, nor to any other Place than that in which the two Houses shall be sitting.

Section. 6.

The Senators and Representatives shall receive a
Compensation for their Services, to be ascertained
by Law, and paid out of the Treasury of the United
States. They shall in all Cases, except Treason, Felony
and Breach of the Peace, be privileged from Arrest
during their Attendance at the Session of their respective Houses, and in going to and returning from the
same; and for any Speech or Debate in either House,
they shall not be questioned in any other Place.

No Senator or Representative shall, during the Time
for which he was elected, be appointed to any civil Office under the Authority of the United States, which
shall have been created, or the Emoluments whereof
shall have been encreased during such time; and no
Person holding any Office under the United States,
shall be a Member of either House during his Continuance in Office.

Section. 7.

All Bills for raising Revenue shall originate in the
House of Representatives; but the Senate may propose
or concur with Amendments as on other Bills.

Every Bill which shall have passed the House of Representatives and the Senate, shall, before it become
a Law, be presented to the President of the United
States: If he approve he shall sign it, but if not he
shall return it, with his Objections to that House in
which it shall have originated, who shall enter the
Objections at large on their Journal, and proceed to
reconsider it. If after such Reconsideration two thirds
of that House shall agree to pass the Bill, it shall be
sent, together with the Objections, to the other House,
by which it shall likewise be reconsidered, and if ap-

proved by two thirds of that House, it shall become a
Law. But in all such Cases the Votes of both Houses
shall be determined by yeas and Nays, and the Names
of the Persons voting for and against the Bill shall be
entered on the Journal of each House respectively. If
any Bill shall not be returned by the President within
ten Days (Sundays excepted) after it shall have been
presented to him, the Same shall be a Law, in like
Manner as if he had signed it, unless the Congress by
their Adjournment prevent its Return, in which Case
it shall not be a Law.

Every Order, Resolution, or Vote to which the Concurrence of the Senate and House of Representatives may
be necessary (except on a question of Adjournment)
shall be presented to the President of the United
States; and before the Same shall take Effect, shall be
approved by him, or being disapproved by him, shall
be repassed by two thirds of the Senate and House of
Representatives, according to the Rules and Limita-
tions prescribed in the Case of a Bill.

Section. 8.
The Congress shall have Power To lay and collect
Taxes, Duties, Imposts and Excises, to pay the Debts
and provide for the common Defence and general
Welfare of the United States; but all Duties, Imposts
and Excises shall be uniform throughout the United
States;
To borrow Money on the credit of the United States;
To regulate Commerce with foreign Nations, and
among the several States, and with the Indian Tribes;
To establish an uniform Rule of Naturalization, and
uniform Laws on the subject of Bankruptcies through-
out the United States;
To coin Money, regulate the Value thereof, and of

foreign Coin, and fix the Standard of Weights and
Measures;

To provide for the Punishment of counterfeiting the
Securities and current Coin of the United States;

To establish Post Offices and post Roads;

To promote the Progress of Science and useful Arts, by
securing for limited Times to Authors and Inventors
the exclusive Right to their respective Writings and
Discoveries;

To constitute Tribunals inferior to the supreme Court;

To define and punish Piracies and Felonies committed on the high Seas, and Offences against the Law of
Nations;

To declare War, grant Letters of Marque and Reprisal,
and make Rules concerning Captures on Land and
Water;

To raise and support Armies, but no Appropriation of
Money to that Use shall be for a longer Term than two
Years;

To provide and maintain a Navy;

To make Rules for the Government and Regulation of
the land and naval Forces;

To provide for calling forth the Militia to execute the
Laws of the Union, suppress Insurrections and repel
Invasions;

To provide for organizing, arming, and disciplining,
the Militia, and for governing such Part of them as
may be employed in the Service of the United States,
reserving to the States respectively, the Appointment
of the Officers, and the Authority of training the Militia according to the discipline prescribed by Congress;

To exercise exclusive Legislation in all Cases what-
soever, over such District (not exceeding ten Miles
square) as may, by Cession of particular States, and
the Acceptance of Congress, become the Seat of the
Government of the United States, and to exercise like

Authority over all Places purchased by the Consent of
the Legislature of the State in which the Same shall
be, for the Erection of Forts, Magazines, Arsenals,
dock-Yards, and other needful Buildings; --And
To make all Laws which shall be necessary and proper
for carrying into Execution the foregoing Powers, and
all other Powers vested by this Constitution in the
Government of the United States, or in any Department or Officer thereof.

Section. 9.
The Migration or Importation of such Persons as any
of the States now existing shall think proper to admit,
shall not be prohibited by the Congress prior to the
Year one thousand eight hundred and eight, but a
Tax or duty may be imposed on such Importation, not
exceeding ten dollars for each Person.
The Privilege of the Writ of Habeas Corpus shall not
be suspended, unless when in Cases of Rebellion or
Invasion the public Safety may require it.

No Bill of Attainder or ex post facto Law shall be
passed.

No Capitation, or other direct, Tax shall be laid,
unless in Proportion to the Census or enumeration
herein before directed to be taken.
No Tax or Duty shall be laid on Articles exported from
any State.
No Preference shall be given by any Regulation of
Commerce or Revenue to the Ports of one State over
those of another; nor shall Vessels bound to, or from,
one State, be obliged to enter, clear, or pay Duties in
another.
No Money shall be drawn from the Treasury, but in
Consequence of Appropriations made by Law; and a

regular Statement and Account of the Receipts and Expenditures of all public Money shall be published from time to time.

No Title of Nobility shall be granted by the United States: And no Person holding any Office of Profit or Trust under them, shall, without the Consent of the Congress, accept of any present, Emolument, Office, or Title, of any kind whatever, from any King, Prince, or foreign State.

Section. 10.
No State shall enter into any Treaty, Alliance, or Confederation; grant Letters of Marque and Reprisal; coin Money; emit Bills of Credit; make any Thing but gold and silver Coin a Tender in Payment of Debts; pass any Bill of Attainder, ex post facto Law, or Law impairing the Obligation of Contracts, or grant any Title of Nobility.

No State shall, without the Consent of the Congress, lay any Imposts or Duties on Imports or Exports, except what may be absolutely necessary for executing it's inspection Laws: and the net Produce of all Duties and Imposts, laid by any State on Imports or Exports, shall be for the Use of the Treasury of the United States; and all such Laws shall be subject to the Revision and Controul of the Congress.

No State shall, without the Consent of Congress, lay any Duty of Tonnage, keep Troops, or Ships of War in time of Peace, enter into any Agreement or Compact with another State, or with a foreign Power, or engage in War, unless actually invaded, or in such imminent Danger as will not admit of delay.

Article. II.
Section. 1.
The executive Power shall be vested in a President of
the United States of America. He shall hold his Office
during the Term of four Years, and, together with the
Vice President, chosen for the same Term, be elected,
as follows:

Each State shall appoint, in such Manner as the
Legislature thereof may direct, a Number of Electors,
equal to the whole Number of Senators and Representatives to which the State may be entitled in the
Congress: but no Senator or Representative, or Person
holding an Office of Trust or Profit under the United
States, shall be appointed an Elector.

The Electors shall meet in their respective States,
and vote by Ballot for two Persons, of whom one at
least shall not be an Inhabitant of the same State
with themselves. And they shall make a List of all
the Persons voted for, and of the Number of Votes
for each; which List they shall sign and certify, and
transmit sealed to the Seat of the Government of the
United States, directed to the President of the Senate. The President of the Senate shall, in the Presence
of the Senate and House of Representatives, open all
the Certificates, and the Votes shall then be counted.
The Person having the greatest Number of Votes shall
be the President, if such Number be a Majority of the
whole Number of Electors appointed; and if there be
more than one who have such Majority, and have an
equal Number of Votes, then the House of Representatives shall immediately chuse by Ballot one of them for
President; and if no Person have a Majority, then from
the five highest on the List the said House shall in like
Manner chuse the President. But in chusing the

President, the Votes shall be taken by States, the Representation from each State having one Vote; A quorum for this purpose shall consist of a Member or Members from two thirds of the States, and a Majority of all the States shall be necessary to a Choice. In every Case, after the Choice of the President, the Person having the greatest Number of Votes of the Electors shall be the Vice President. But if there should remain two or more who have equal Votes, the Senate shall chuse from them by Ballot the Vice President.

The Congress may determine the Time of chusing the Electors, and the Day on which they shall give their Votes; which Day shall be the same throughout the United States.

No Person except a natural born Citizen, or a Citizen of the United States, at the time of the Adoption of this Constitution, shall be eligible to the Office of President; neither shall any Person be eligible to that Office who shall not have attained to the Age of thirty five Years, and been fourteen Years a Resident within the United States.

In Case of the Removal of the President from Office, or of his Death, Resignation, or Inability to discharge the Powers and Duties of the said Office, the Same shall devolve on the Vice President, and the Congress may by Law provide for the Case of Removal, Death, Resignation or Inability, both of the President and Vice President, declaring what Officer shall then act as President, and such Officer shall act accordingly, until the Disability be removed, or a President shall be elected.

The President shall, at stated Times, receive for his Services, a Compensation, which shall neither be

increased nor diminished during the Period for which
he shall have been elected, and he shall not receive
within that Period any other Emolument from the
United States, or any of them.
Before he enter on the Execution of his Office, he shall
take the following Oath or Affirmation: --"I do solemn-
ly swear (or affirm) that I will faithfully execute the
Office of President of the United States, and will to the
best of my Ability, preserve, protect and defend the
Constitution of the United States."

Section. 2.
The President shall be Commander in Chief of the
Army and Navy of the United States, and of the Militia of the several States, when called into the actual Service of the United States; he may require the
Opinion, in writing, of the principal Officer in each of
the executive Departments, upon any Subject relating
to the Duties of their respective Offices, and he shall
have Power to grant Reprieves and Pardons for Offences against the United States, except in Cases of
Impeachment.
He shall have Power, by and with the Advice and
Consent of the Senate, to make Treaties, provided two
thirds of the Senators present concur; and he shall
nominate, and by and with the Advice and Consent of
the Senate, shall appoint Ambassadors, other public
Ministers and Consuls, Judges of the supreme Court,
and all other Officers of the United States, whose Appointments are not herein otherwise provided for, and
which shall be established by Law: but the Congress
may by Law vest the Appointment of such inferior Officers, as they think proper, in the President alone, in
the Courts of Law, or in the Heads of Departments.
The President shall have Power to fill up all Vacancies
that may happen during the Recess of the Senate, by

granting Commissions which shall expire at the End of their next Session.

Section. 3.
He shall from time to time give to the Congress Information of the State of the Union, and recommend to their Consideration such Measures as he shall judge necessary and expedient; he may, on extraordinary Occasions, convene both Houses, or either of them, and in Case of Disagreement between them, with Respect to the Time of Adjournment, he may adjourn them to such Time as he shall think proper; he shall receive Ambassadors and other public Ministers; he shall take Care that the Laws be faithfully executed, and shall Commission all the Officers of the United States.

Section. 4.
The President, Vice President and all civil Officers of the United States, shall be removed from Office on Impeachment for, and Conviction of, Treason, Bribery, or other high Crimes and Misdemeanors.

Article III.
Section. 1.
The judicial Power of the United States shall be vested in one supreme Court, and in such inferior Courts as the Congress may from time to time ordain and establish. The Judges, both of the supreme and inferior Courts, shall hold their Offices during good Behaviour, and shall, at stated Times, receive for their Services a Compensation, which shall not be diminished during their Continuance in Office.

Section. 2.

The judicial Power shall extend to all Cases, in Law and Equity, arising under this Constitution, the Laws of the United States, and Treaties made, or which shall be made, under their Authority;--to all Cases affecting Ambassadors, other public Ministers and Consuls;--to all Cases of admiralty and maritime Jurisdiction;--to Controversies to which the United States shall be a Party;--to Controversies between two or more States;-- between a State and Citizens of another State;--between Citizens of different States;--between Citizens of the same State claiming Lands under Grants of different States, and between a State, or the Citizens thereof, and foreign States, Citizens or Subjects.

In all Cases affecting Ambassadors, other public Ministers and Consuls, and those in which a State shall be Party, the supreme Court shall have original Jurisdiction. In all the other Cases before mentioned, the supreme Court shall have appellate Jurisdiction, both as to Law and Fact, with such Exceptions, and under such Regulations as the Congress shall make.

The Trial of all Crimes, except in Cases of Impeachment, shall be by Jury; and such Trial shall be held in the State where the said Crimes shall have been committed; but when not committed within any State, the Trial shall be at such Place or Places as the Congress may by Law have directed.

Section. 3.

Treason against the United States, shall consist only in levying War against them, or in adhering to their Enemies, giving them Aid and Comfort. No Person shall be convicted of Treason unless on the Testimony of two Witnesses to the same overt Act, or on Confession in open Court.

The Congress shall have Power to declare the Punishment of Treason, but no Attainder of Treason shall work Corruption of Blood, or Forfeiture except during the Life of the Person attainted.

Article. IV.
Section. 1.
Full Faith and Credit shall be given in each State to the public Acts, Records, and judicial Proceedings of every other State. And the Congress may by general Laws prescribe the Manner in which such Acts, Records and Proceedings shall be proved, and the Effect thereof.

Section. 2.
The Citizens of each State shall be entitled to all Privileges and Immunities of Citizens in the several States.

A Person charged in any State with Treason, Felony, or other Crime, who shall flee from Justice, and be found in another State, shall on Demand of the executive Authority of the State from which he fled, be delivered up, to be removed to the State having Jurisdiction of the Crime.
No Person held to Service or Labour in one State, under the Laws thereof, escaping into another, shall, in Consequence of any Law or Regulation therein, be discharged from such Service or Labour, but shall be delivered up on Claim of the Party to whom such Service or Labour may be due.

Section. 3.
New States may be admitted by the Congress into this Union; but no new State shall be formed or erected within the Jurisdiction of any other State; nor any

State be formed by the Junction of two or more States, or Parts of States, without the Consent of the Legislatures of the States concerned as well as of the Congress.

The Congress shall have Power to dispose of and make all needful Rules and Regulations respecting the Territory or other Property belonging to the United States; and nothing in this Constitution shall be so construed as to Prejudice any Claims of the United States, or of any particular State.

Section. 4.
The United States shall guarantee to every State in this Union a Republican Form of Government, and shall protect each of them against Invasion; and on Application of the Legislature, or of the Executive (when the Legislature cannot be convened), against domestic Violence.

Article. V.
The Congress, whenever two thirds of both Houses shall deem it necessary, shall propose Amendments to this Constitution, or, on the Application of the Legislatures of two thirds of the several States, shall call a Convention for proposing Amendments, which, in either Case, shall be valid to all Intents and Purposes, as Part of this Constitution, when ratified by the Legislatures of three fourths of the several States, or by Conventions in three fourths thereof, as the one or the other Mode of Ratification may be proposed by the Congress; Provided that no Amendment which may be made prior to the Year One thousand eight hundred and eight shall in any Manner affect the first and fourth Clauses in the Ninth Section of the first Article; and that no State, without its Consent, shall be deprived of its equal Suffrage in the Senate.

Article. VI.

All Debts contracted and Engagements entered into, before the Adoption of this Constitution, shall be as valid against the United States under this Constitution, as under the Confederation.

This Constitution, and the Laws of the United States which shall be made in Pursuance thereof; and all Treaties made, or which shall be made, under the Authority of the United States, shall be the supreme Law of the Land; and the Judges in every State shall be bound thereby, any Thing in the Constitution or Laws of any State to the Contrary notwithstanding.

The Senators and Representatives before mentioned, and the Members of the several State Legislatures, and all executive and judicial Officers, both of the United States and of the several States, shall be bound by Oath or Affirmation, to support this Constitution; but no religious Test shall ever be required as a Qualification to any Office or public Trust under the United States.

Article. VII.

The Ratification of the Conventions of nine States, shall be sufficient for the Establishment of this Constitution between the States so ratifying the Same.

The Word, "the," being interlined between the seventh and eighth Lines of the first Page, the Word "Thirty" being partly written on an Erazure in the fifteenth Line of the first Page, The Words "is tried" being interlined between the thirty second and thirty third Lines of the first Page and the Word "the" being interlined between the forty third and forty fourth Lines of the second Page.

Attest William Jackson Secretary

Done in Convention by the Unanimous Consent of the States present the Seventeenth Day of September in the Year of our Lord one thousand seven hundred and Eighty seven and of the Independence of the United States of America the Twelfth In witness whereof We have hereunto subscribed our Names,

G°. Washington, Presidt and deputy from Virginia
Delaware: Geo: Read, Gunning Bedford jun, John Dickinson, Richard Bassett, Jaco: Broom
Maryland: James McHenry, Dan of St Thos. Jenifer, Danl. Carroll
Virginia:John Blair, James Madison Jr.
North Carolina:Wm. Blount, Richd. Dobbs Spaight, Hu Williamson
South Carolina:J. Rutledge, Charles Cotesworth Pinckney, Charles Pinckney:
Pierce Butler
Georgia:William Few, Abr Baldwin
New Hampshire:John Langdon, Nicholas Gilman
Massachusetts:Nathaniel Gorham, Rufus King
Connecticut:Wm. Saml. Johnson, Roger Sherman
New York:Alexander Hamilton
New Jersey:Wil: Livingston, David Brearley, Wm. Paterson, Jona: Dayton
Pennsylvania:B Franklin, Thomas Mifflin, Robt. Morris, Geo. Clymer,
Thos. FitzSimons, Jared Ingersoll, James Wilson, Gouv Morris

Appendix

Number Two:

The Bill of Rights,

containing all

the amendments

to the Constitution -

thus far.

The Preamble to The Bill of Rights
Congress of the United States begun and held at the City
of New-York, on Wednesday the fourth of March, one thousand seven hundred and eighty nine.

THE Conventions of a number of the States, having at the
time of their adopting the Constitution, expressed a desire,
in order to prevent misconstruction or abuse of its powers,
that further declaratory and restrictive clauses should be
added: And as extending the ground of public confidence in
the Government, will best ensure the beneficent ends of its
institution.

RESOLVED by the Senate and House of Representatives of
the United States of America, in Congress assembled, two
thirds of both Houses concurring, that the following Articles
be proposed to the Legislatures of the several States, as
amendments to the Constitution of the United States, all, or
any of which Articles, when ratified by three fourths of the
said Legislatures, to be valid to all intents and purposes, as
part of the said Constitution; viz.

ARTICLES in addition to, and Amendment of the Constitution of the United States of America, proposed by Congress,
and ratified by the Legislatures of the several States, pursu-
ant to the fifth Article of the original Constitution.

Note: The following is a transcription of the first ten amendments to the Constitution in their original form. These
amendments were ratified December 15, 1791, and form
what is known as the "Bill of Rights."

Amendment I
Congress shall make no law respecting an establishment of
religion, or prohibiting the free exercise thereof; or abridg-
ing the freedom of speech, or of the press; or the right of the
people peaceably to assemble, and to petition the Government for a redress of grievances.

Amendment II
A well regulated Militia, being necessary to the security of a free State, the right of the people to keep and bear Arms, shall not be infringed.

Amendment III
No Soldier shall, in time of peace be quartered in any house, without the consent of the Owner, nor in time of war, but in a manner to be prescribed by law.

Amendment IV
The right of the people to be secure in their persons, houses, papers, and effects, against unreasonable searches and seizures, shall not be violated, and no Warrants shall issue, but upon probable cause, supported by Oath or affirmation, and particularly describing the place to be searched, and the persons or things to be seized.

Amendment V
No person shall be held to answer for a capital, or otherwise infamous crime, unless on a presentment or indictment of a Grand Jury, except in cases arising in the land or naval forces, or in the Militia, when in actual service in time of War or public danger; nor shall any person be subject for the same offence to be twice put in jeopardy of life or limb; nor shall be compelled in any criminal case to be a witness against himself, nor be deprived of life, liberty, or property, without due process of law; nor shall private property be taken for public use, without just compensation.

Amendment VI
In all criminal prosecutions, the accused shall enjoy the right to a speedy and public trial, by an impartial jury of the State and district wherein the crime shall have been committed, which district shall have been previously ascertained by law, and to be informed of the nature and cause of the accusation; to be confronted with the witnesses against him; to have compulsory process for obtaining witnesses

in his favor, and to have the Assistance of Counsel for his defence.

Amendment VII
In Suits at common law, where the value in controversy shall exceed twenty dollars, the right of trial by jury shall be preserved, and no fact tried by a jury, shall be otherwise re-examined in any Court of the United States, than according to the rules of the common law.

Amendment VIII
Excessive bail shall not be required, nor excessive fines imposed, nor cruel and unusual punishments inflicted.

Amendment IX
The enumeration in the Constitution, of certain rights, shall not be construed to deny or disparage others retained by the people.

Amendment X
The powers not delegated to the United States by the Constitution, nor prohibited by it to the States, are reserved to the States respectively, or to the people.

AMENDMENT XI
Passed by Congress March 4, 1794. Ratified February 7, 1795.
Note: Article III, section 2, of the Constitution was modified by amendment 11.
The Judicial power of the United States shall not be construed to extend to any suit in law or equity, commenced or prosecuted against one of the United States by Citizens of another State, or by Citizens or Subjects of any Foreign State.

AMENDMENT XII

Passed by Congress December 9, 1803. Ratified June 15, 1804.

Note: A portion of Article II, section 1 of the Constitution was superseded by the 12th amendment.

The Electors shall meet in their respective states and vote by ballot for President and Vice-President, one of whom, at least, shall not be an inhabitant of the same state with themselves; they shall name in their ballots the person voted for as President, and in distinct ballots the person voted for as Vice-President, and they shall make distinct lists of all persons voted for as President, and of all persons voted for as Vice-President, and of the number of votes for each, which lists they shall sign and certify, and transmit sealed to the seat of the government of the United States, directed to the President of the Senate; -- the President of the Senate shall, in the presence of the Senate and House of Representatives, open all the certificates and the votes shall then be counted; -- The person having the greatest number of votes for President, shall be the President, if such number be a majority of the whole number of Electors appointed; and if no person have such majority, then from the persons having the highest numbers not exceeding three on the list of those voted for as President, the House of Representatives shall choose immediately, by ballot, the President. But in choosing the President, the votes shall be taken by states, the representation from each state having one vote; a quorum for this purpose shall consist of a member or members from two-thirds of the states, and a majority of all the states shall be necessary to a choice. [And if the House of Representatives shall not choose a President whenever the right of choice shall devolve upon them, before the fourth day of March next following, then the Vice-President shall act as President, as in case of the death or other constitutional disability of the President. --]* The person having the greatest number of votes as Vice-President, shall be the Vice-President, if such number be a majority of the whole number of Electors appointed, and if no person have a majority, then from the two highest numbers on the list, the Senate shall

choose the Vice-President; a quorum for the purpose shall consist of two-thirds of the whole number of Senators, and a majority of the whole number shall be necessary to a choice. But no person constitutionally ineligible to the office of President shall be eligible to that of Vice-President of the United States.
*Superseded by section 3 of the 20th amendment.

AMENDMENT XIII
Passed by Congress January 31, 1865. Ratified December 6, 1865.
Note: A portion of Article IV, section 2, of the Constitution was superseded by the 13th amendment.
Section 1. Neither slavery nor involuntary servitude, except as a punishment for crime whereof the party shall have been duly convicted, shall exist within the United States, or any place subject to their jurisdiction.
Section 2. Congress shall have power to enforce this article by appropriate legislation.

AMENDMENT XIV
Passed by Congress June 13, 1866. Ratified July 9, 1868.
Note: Article I, section 2, of the Constitution was modified by section 2 of the 14th amendment.
Section 1. All persons born or naturalized in the United States, and subject to the jurisdiction thereof, are citizens of the United States and of the State wherein they reside. No State shall make or enforce any law which shall abridge the privileges or immunities of citizens of the United States; nor shall any State deprive any person of life, liberty, or property, without due process of law; nor deny to any person within its jurisdiction the equal protection of the laws.
Section 2. Representatives shall be apportioned among the several States according to their respective numbers, counting the whole number of persons in each State, excluding Indians not taxed. But when the right to vote at any election for the choice of electors for President and Vice-President of the United States, Representatives in Congress, the

Executive and Judicial officers of a State, or the members of the Legislature thereof, is denied to any of the male inhabitants of such State, being twenty-one years of age,* and citizens of the United States, or in any way abridged, except for participation in rebellion, or other crime, the basis of representation therein shall be reduced in the proportion which the number of such male citizens shall bear to the whole number of male citizens twenty-one years of age in such State.

Section 3. No person shall be a Senator or Representative in Congress, or elector of President and Vice-President, or hold any office, civil or military, under the United States, or under any State, who, having previously taken an oath, as a member of Congress, or as an officer of the United States, or as a member of any State legislature, or as an executive or judicial officer of any State, to support the Constitution of the United States, shall have engaged in insurrection or rebellion against the same, or given aid or comfort to the enemies thereof. But Congress may by a vote of two-thirds of each House, remove such disability.

Section 4. The validity of the public debt of the United States, authorized by law, including debts incurred for payment of pensions and bounties for services in suppressing insurrection or rebellion, shall not be questioned. But neither the United States nor any State shall assume or pay any debt or obligation incurred in aid of insurrection or rebellion against the United States, or any claim for the loss or emancipation of any slave; but all such debts, obligations and claims shall be held illegal and void.

Section 5. The Congress shall have the power to enforce, by appropriate legislation, the provisions of this article.

*Changed by section 1 of the 26th amendment.

AMENDMENT XV

Passed by Congress February 26, 1869. Ratified February 3, 1870.

Section 1. The right of citizens of the United States to vote shall not be denied or abridged by the United States or by any State on account of race, color, or previous condition of

servitude--
Section 2. The Congress shall have the power to enforce this article by appropriate legislation.

AMENDMENT XVI
Passed by Congress July 2, 1909. Ratified February 3, 1913.
Note: Article I, section 9, of the Constitution was modified by amendment 16.
The Congress shall have power to lay and collect taxes on incomes, from whatever source derived, without apportionment among the several States, and without regard to any census or enumeration.

AMENDMENT XVII
Passed by Congress May 13, 1912. Ratified April 8, 1913.
Note: Article I, section 3, of the Constitution was modified by the 17th amendment.
The Senate of the United States shall be composed of two Senators from each State, elected by the people thereof, for six years; and each Senator shall have one vote. The electors in each State shall have the qualifications requisite for electors of the most numerous branch of the State legislatures.
When vacancies happen in the representation of any State in the Senate, the executive authority of such State shall issue writs of election to fill such vacancies: Provided, That the legislature of any State may empower the executive thereof to make temporary appointments until the people fill the vacancies by election as the legislature may direct.

This amendment shall not be so construed as to affect the election or term of any Senator chosen before it becomes valid as part of the Constitution.

AMENDMENT XVIII
Passed by Congress December 18, 1917. Ratified January 16, 1919. Repealed by amendment 21.
Section 1. After one year from the ratification of this article the manufacture, sale, or transportation of intoxicating

liquors within, the importation thereof into, or the exportation thereof from the United States and all territory subject to the jurisdiction thereof for beverage purposes is hereby prohibited.

Section 2. The Congress and the several States shall have concurrent power to enforce this article by appropriate legislation.

Section 3. This article shall be inoperative unless it shall have been ratified as an amendment to the Constitution by the legislatures of the several States, as provided in the Constitution, within seven years from the date of the submission hereof to the States by the Congress.

AMENDMENT XIX

Passed by Congress June 4, 1919. Ratified August 18, 1920.

The right of citizens of the United States to vote shall not be denied or abridged by the United States or by any State on account of sex.

Congress shall have power to enforce this article by appropriate legislation.

AMENDMENT XX

Passed by Congress March 2, 1932. Ratified January 23, 1933.

Note: Article I, section 4, of the Constitution was modified by section 2 of this amendment. In addition, a portion of the 12th amendment was superseded by section 3.

Section 1. The terms of the President and the Vice President shall end at noon on the 20th day of January, and the terms of Senators and Representatives at noon on the 3d day of January, of the years in which such terms would have ended if this article had not been ratified; and the terms of their successors shall then begin.

Section 2. The Congress shall assemble at least once in every year, and such meeting shall begin at noon on the 3d day of January, unless they shall by law appoint a different day.

Section 3. If, at the time fixed for the beginning of the term of the President, the President elect shall have died, the

Vice President elect shall become President. If a President shall not have been chosen before the time fixed for the beginning of his term, or if the President elect shall have failed to qualify, then the Vice President elect shall act as President until a President shall have qualified; and the Congress may by law provide for the case wherein neither a President elect nor a Vice President shall have qualified, declaring who shall then act as President, or the manner in which one who is to act shall be selected, and such person shall act accordingly until a President or Vice President shall have qualified.

Section 4. The Congress may by law provide for the case of the death of any of the persons from whom the House of Representatives may choose a President whenever the right of choice shall have devolved upon them, and for the case of the death of any of the persons from whom the Senate may choose a Vice President whenever the right of choice shall have devolved upon them.

Section 5. Sections 1 and 2 shall take effect on the 15th day of October following the ratification of this article.

Section 6. This article shall be inoperative unless it shall have been ratified as an amendment to the Constitution by the legislatures of three-fourths of the several States within seven years from the date of its submission.

AMENDMENT XXI

Passed by Congress February 20, 1933. Ratified December 5, 1933.

Section 1. The eighteenth article of amendment to the Constitution of the United States is hereby repealed.

Section 2. The transportation or importation into any State, Territory, or Possession of the United States for delivery or use therein of intoxicating liquors, in violation of the laws thereof, is hereby prohibited.

Section 3. This article shall be inoperative unless it shall have been ratified as an amendment to the Constitution by conventions in the several States, as provided in the Constitution, within seven years from the date of the submission hereof to the States by the Congress.

AMENDMENT XXII
Passed by Congress March 21, 1947. Ratified February 27, 1951.
Section 1. No person shall be elected to the office of the President more than twice, and no person who has held the office of President, or acted as President, for more than two years of a term to which some other person was elected President shall be elected to the office of President more than once. But this Article shall not apply to any person holding the office of President when this Article was proposed by Congress, and shall not prevent any person who may be holding the office of President, or acting as President, during the term within which this Article becomes operative from holding the office of President or acting as President during the remainder of such term.
Section 2. This article shall be inoperative unless it shall have been ratified as an amendment to the Constitution by the legislatures of three-fourths of the several States within seven years from the date of its submission to the States by the Congress.

AMENDMENT XXIII
Passed by Congress June 16, 1960. Ratified March 29, 1961.
Section 1. The District constituting the seat of Government of the United States shall appoint in such manner as Congress may direct:
A number of electors of President and Vice President equal to the whole number of Senators and Representatives in Congress to which the District would be entitled if it were a State, but in no event more than the least populous State; they shall be in addition to those appointed by the States, but they shall be considered, for the purposes of the election of President and Vice President, to be electors appointed by a State; and they shall meet in the District and perform such duties as provided by the twelfth article of amendment.

Section 2. The Congress shall have power to enforce this

article by appropriate legislation.

AMENDMENT XXIV
Passed by Congress August 27, 1962. Ratified January 23, 1964.
Section 1. The right of citizens of the United States to vote in any primary or other election for President or Vice President, for electors for President or Vice President, or for Senator or Representative in Congress, shall not be denied or abridged by the United States or any State by reason of failure to pay poll tax or other tax.
Section 2. The Congress shall have power to enforce this article by appropriate legislation.

AMENDMENT XXV
Passed by Congress July 6, 1965. Ratified February 10, 1967.
Note: Article II, section 1, of the Constitution was affected by the 25th amendment.
Section 1. In case of the removal of the President from office or of his death or resignation, the Vice President shall become President.
Section 2. Whenever there is a vacancy in the office of the Vice President, the President shall nominate a Vice President who shall take office upon confirmation by a majority vote of both Houses of Congress.
Section 3. Whenever the President transmits to the President pro tempore of the Senate and the Speaker of the House of Representatives his written declaration that he is unable to discharge the powers and duties of his office, and until he transmits to them a written declaration to the contrary, such powers and duties shall be discharged by the Vice President as Acting President.
Section 4. Whenever the Vice President and a majority of either the principal officers of the executive departments or of such other body as Congress may by law provide, transmit to the President pro tempore of the Senate and the Speaker of the House of Representatives their written declaration that the President is unable to discharge the powers and

duties of his office, the Vice President shall immediately assume the powers and duties of the office as Acting President.

Thereafter, when the President transmits to the President pro tempore of the Senate and the Speaker of the House of Representatives his written declaration that no inability exists, he shall resume the powers and duties of his office unless the Vice President and a majority of either the principal officers of the executive department or of such other body as Congress may by law provide, transmit within four days to the President pro tempore of the Senate and the Speaker of the House of Representatives their written declaration that the President is unable to discharge the powers and duties of his office. Thereupon Congress shall decide the issue, assembling within forty-eight hours for that purpose if not in session. If the Congress, within twenty-one days after receipt of the latter written declaration, or, if Congress is not in session, within twenty-one days after Congress is required to assemble, determines by two-thirds vote of both Houses that the President is unable to discharge the powers and duties of his office, the Vice President shall continue to discharge the same as Acting President; otherwise, the President shall resume the powers and duties of his office.

AMENDMENT XXVI
Passed by Congress March 23, 1971. Ratified July 1, 1971.
Note: Amendment 14, section 2, of the Constitution was modified by section 1 of the 26th amendment.
Section 1. The right of citizens of the United States, who are eighteen years of age or older, to vote shall not be denied or abridged by the United States or by any State on account of age.
Section 2. The Congress shall have power to enforce this article by appropriate legislation.

AMENDMENT XXVII
Originally proposed Sept. 25, 1789. Ratified May 7, 1992.
No law, varying the compensation for the services of the
Senators and Representatives, shall take effect, until an
election of representatives shall have intervened.

Appendix Number Three:
Now that you've got the hang of it.

Here's where you can take your cue from Thomas Jefferson and company and pen your own suggestions for improving this magnificent, if flawed, Constitution of ours.

The following pages are provided for you to express your own ideas of what would make for a more perfect union.

My Amendment #1:

_____

_____

_____

_____

_____

_____

_____

_____

_____ .

_____

_____

My Amendment #2:

_____

_____

_____

_____

_____

_____

_____

_____

_____

_____.

_____

_____

My Amendment #3:

_____

_____

My Amendment #4:

_____

_____

My Amendment #5:

_____

_____

_____

_____

_____

_____

_____

_____

_____

_____

_____.

_____

_____

My Amendment #6:

_____

_____

_____

_____

_____

_____

_____

_____

_____.

_____

_____

Appendix

Number Four:

Time to light

the fuse.

After you've taken matters into your own hands comes the crucial step of getting your voice heard. It's simple and effective, especially if a couple hundred million of us do it at the same time.

Here's how:

First, write your Congressman.
Then your Senator.
Then visit their office personally.
Then stage a peaceful
protest outside their home.
Then grab a musket.

Here's where to go to find their address:

http://www.senate.gov/general/contact_
information/senators_cfm.cfm

http://www.visi.com/juan/congress/

The standard formula to use for addressing a letter to a member of Congress is the following:

The Honorable (Full Name)
United States Senate
Room Number and Building
(ex. 123 Russell Senate Office Building)
Washington, D.C. 20510

Dear Senator (Last Name):

Or

The Honorable (Full Name):
United States House of Representatives
Room Number and Building
(ex. 1234 Rayburn House Office Building)
Washington, D.C. 20515
VIA Fax: (202) XXX-XXXX

Dear Representative (Last Name)

Here is a sample letter to a prominent legislator:

The Honorable Joseph Lieberman
706 Hart Senate Office Building
Washington, DC 20510

Dear Senator Lieberman,

Greetings. I am your constituent from _____
_____(your neighborhood here) and am no
longer content to stand aside and let our country
continue its downward spiral towards irrelevancy,
insolvency, and impotency.

Please read the amendments I've enclosed, grab a
gavel and do something to restore public confidence
in our government. Or my friends and I will come
down there and do it for you.

Time is short. We'll give you 30 days to get your
act together.

Respectfully submitted,

John/Judy Q. Public

Thank you, fellow American.

Just by reading this chapbook, you've put your patriotism into action. Please pass your version of democracy on to anyone who will listen. And even if they don't, keep talking. They might eventually come around.

Extra special thanks to Melissa Jun, Chris Ilagan, Brian Rosencrans and Bill Weeden for helping bring democratic principles to light. To Marcy and Jack Henry for exemplifying America at its best. And to Ben and Jane Whitten for raising a politically conscious family near Valley Forge, Pennsylvania.

For more on this and other
relevant social issues, visit
www.vitallyimportant.com

"I'm Rufus King, and I approved this manuscript."

Rufus served our country as a delegate from
Massachusetts to the Constitutional Convention,
in addition to being the Federalist candidate
for President of the United States in 1816.